SHOREBIRDS

Des Thompson and Ingvar Byrkjedal

WORLDLIFE
LIBRARY

Voyageur Press

Contents

Photograph opposite: American oystercatcher

Page 1 photograph: Black-necked stilt   Page 3 photograph: Common greenshank eggs

Introduction

The restlessness of shorebirds, their kinship with the distance and swift seasons,
the wistful signal of their voices down the long coastlines of the world make them, for me,
the most affecting of wild creatures. I think of them as birds of the wind, as 'wind birds'. To the
traveler confounded by exotic birds, not to speak of exotic specimens of his own kind,
the voice of the wind birds may be the lone familiar note in a strange land,
and I have many times been glad to find them…

Peter Matthiessen, *The Shorebirds of North America* (1967)

There are moments in one's life when time stands still. We have experienced many of these in the company of shorebirds. Crouching on windswept mountain plateaux; exposed to the rawest elements of the arctic tundra; drenched in vast peatland plains; chilled by the bracing winds on a coastal mudflat; or merely sitting by pasture fields, we have been in contact with one of the most beautiful and enchanting forms of life on land – the shorebirds.

It's not just the color and form that excite us, for while most shorebirds are gloriously striking, some are quite drab. No, it's much more than this; our pleasure has been in absorbing their intoxicating sounds, their astonishingly varied behavior and habits on the ground and in the air; their affinity with so many faraway places, the amazing journeys they make to and from these places, and the sheer *joie de vivre* that they instil in the watcher.

We have experienced these encounters in a variety of places: on a beautiful June evening walk close to Hudson Bay, Canada, listening to Hudsonian godwits, whimbrel and American golden plovers; peering at a lone common greenshank, calling on one of thousands of boulders half a mile (800 meters) away, before he exchanges duties with his mate on the nest; marveling at the acrobatic song flights of northern lapwings accompanied by their characteristic 'wee-ip' calls; and watching tight flocks of thousands of knot and

Male American avocet on its breeding grounds hunting for invertebrates below the water.

dunlin racing overhead, as they twist and turn, up and down, propelled at breakneck speed against the backdrop of some murky, industrial conurbation. Some of these glimpses were one-offs; others are regular occurrences, seen in the fields when taking the children to school, or while walking by the sea.

Just think about where these birds have been, their adaptations to a challenging environment, and the complex lives they lead. Think about the sanderling running in and out of the waves lapping on the sandy shore; some of these nest on the lands closest to the North Pole, yet migrate to spend winter as far south as Tierra del Fuego. Other shorebirds, such as white-rumped sandpipers, curlew sandpipers and American golden plovers, also make phenomenal journeys between the two hemispheres – yet many individuals return to nest in the same spot year after year!

Eurasian golden plover signaling danger.

We have watched these birds throughout most of our lives. Ingvar's first encounter was with a flock of Eurasian golden plovers in a field in Jaeren, Norway, spied as he was cycling past. The doyen of shorebird watchers, Desmond Nethersole-Thompson, took a small boy barely able to walk (Des) across vast tracts of bogland, surrounded by high mountains, in north Scotland, to see his first nesting greenshanks, dunlins, common sandpipers and golden plovers. Much later, we met in Norway to begin work on our first book, *Tundra Plovers*.

We are utterly convinced that shorebirds are among the most interesting, puzzling and challenging of all life forms. They offer a delightful spectacle – agile, exciting, unpredictable, beautiful and tantalizing.

Mixed flock of dunlin, ringed plovers and turnstones.

Diverse Families

As a whole, the shorebirds (or 'waders', as they are popularly known in Europe) are long-legged, and tend to be associated with the shore, marshes, bogs or other predominantly wet areas. Many of them migrate over long distances – the definitive globe trotters. A close look reveals a tremendous variety of plumages, bill sizes and shapes, vocabulary and behavior patterns. Virtually all species nest on the ground, many making just a scrape, with most clutches consisting of four, cryptically patterned eggs. On hatching, the young leave the nest almost immediately, or within a couple of hours, and are cared for by both parents, though the female tends to desert before the male. Each of these aspects differs between species, however, and there are many exceptions to even the simple biological rules.

There are 199 species of shorebirds. The greatest number of nesting species occurs in Asia (90 species), followed by North America (52), Eurasia (41), South America (33) and Africa (33). Australia has only 16 species, but Central America has the fewest of all in the world's regions, with only four nesting shorebird species.

Shorebird classification

All species of animal or plant are classified into a hierarchy. If we take a particular shorebird species, such as the killdeer – common on the open agricultural plains of North America – it belongs to a class (Aves: birds), then an order (Ciconiiformes), then a family (Charadriidae: plovers), and finally a genus (*Charadrius*), within which it has the unique species name *Charadrius vociferus*, its Latin name betraying its vociferous 'kill-dee' call. Each species is classified in this way, though there can be sub-sets of some groups in the hierarchical tree, such as orders subdivided into suborders, infraorders and parvorders; superfamilies subdivided into families; and some species classified further as subspecies.

We have used a new DNA-based classification to group the shorebirds. This was published by Charles Sibley and Jon Ahlquist in their monumental tome *Phylogeny and*

Scolopacids and Charadriids – a flock of phalaropes, with stilts foraging behind nearer the shore.

Classification of Birds: a study of molecular Evolution (1990). According to this, the shorebirds belong to one of the world's largest and most complex orders of birds, the Ciconiiformes.

Going down one step, into the suborder Charadrii, we find two infraorders: one containing just four species of sandgrouse, and the other, a huge one, embracing the other 195 species of true shorebirds. The word Charadrii is derived from the Greek word *charadra*, meaning a gully — one of the coastal habitats where many shorebirds are seen. Further down the shorebird classification we find two large, species-rich lineages. The Scolopacida contains birds which have always been considered shorebirds. The Charadriida, on the other hand, includes several shorebirds, but also gulls, terns, skimmers, skuas, and auks.

Let's look at the families in detail, starting with the largest ones.

The sandpipers

The **sandpipers, snipes, dowitchers, shanks, godwits, curlews, woodcocks, phalaropes** and **turnstones** comprise the largest family (Scolopacidae, the **'sandpiper family'**) with 88 species. Most of these breed in the northern hemisphere in habitats ranging from open steppes, forests and wetlands to tundra in the far north, and most migrate over long distances. These are small to medium-sized birds, 4½ to 26 in (12 to 66 cm), bill to tail tips — the majority having long legs, slender heads and smallish eyes. Their bills tend to be long, and in some species are curved, which equips them well for hunting by touch, rather than by sight.

There are two subfamilies. The first of these, comprising the snipes and woodcocks (Scolopacinae: 25 species), have long, straight bills, fairly short legs with long toes, and constitute a small, uniform group. All of them are superbly camouflaged on the ground because of their upper plumage, consisting of pale buffish markings mixed with darker browns and blacks. Snipes are unusual in that some species perform territorial, non-vocal song flights. While circling their territories the birds regularly swoop down in whizzing dives. Spreading their outermost tail feathers in order to vibrate them in the air stream, these birds emit some of the most weird avian utterances — so-called 'drumming'.

The woodcocks are unusual also, in being birds of twilight (crepuscular) and night, with

The New Classification of Shorebirds

(family groups in bold in box on right are true shorebirds;
the number of species in each family is given on right.)

THE TRUE SHOREBIRDS

PTEROCLIDES
(sandgrouse)

JACANOIDEA

JACANIDAE
(jacanas)   8

ROSTRATULIDAE
(painted snipes)   2

CHARADRII
(all shorebirds, gulls, auks,
skuas and sheathbills)

SCOLOPACIDA

THINOCORIDAE
(seedsnipes)   4

PEDIONOMIDAE
(plains-wanderer)   1

SCOLOPACOIDEA

SCOLOPACIDAE
(woodcocks, snipes,
godwits, curlew,
whimbrel, shanks,
sandpipers, tattlers,
turnstones, dowitchers,
knots, stints
and phalaropes)   88

CICONIIFORMES
(containing wading birds
and many others)

CHARADRIIDES
(true shorebirds, sheath-
bills, gulls, skuas, terns and
auks)

CHARADRIOIDEA

CICONII
(herons, storks, ibises,
raptors and many others)

CHARADRIIDA → CHIONIDOIDEA

BURHINIDAE
(stone curlew, dikkops
and thick-knees)   9

CHARADRIIDAE
(oystercatchers, stilts,
avocets, plovers,
dotterels and
lapwings)   87

LAROIDEA

ORDER   SUBORDER   INFRAORDER   PARVORDER   SUPERFAMILY   FAMILY

males of several species performing roding flights at dawn and dusk to attract females. They nest mainly in damp forests and are superbly cryptic, with reddish-brown backs streaked with black, pale, white or yellow markings, and black bands on the nape.

The other subfamily, the Tringinae, is large and diverse, with several discrete groups of birds. One of these groups has 18 sparrow- to thrush-sized species, usually referred to as sandpipers (*Calidris*). They have a distinctive non-breeding appearance – their white or pale underparts contrasting with a darker gray or brown mantle. Among these are the fascinating arctic shorebirds – great and red knots, sanderling, red-necked and little stints, and the semi-palmated, western, white-rumped, Baird's, pectoral, sharp-tailed, curlew, purple and rock sandpipers.

Common greenshank.

Another group, comprising the shanks, tattlers and close relatives (16 species), has birds with longish, brightly colored legs and long bills, and which tend to be very noisy. These are typically birds of freshwater margins. Intriguingly, at least three species nest in trees, two of them in the old nests of passerines, the third in nests built by the birds themselves.

There are five further groups. The dowitchers (three species) and godwits (four species) are readily recognized, being tall, with long, straight or slightly upturned bills. They have a more or less coppery colored breeding plumage. Curlews (eight species) are the largest of shorebirds. They are brown-spotted and have long, down-curved bills. Related to these is the upland sandpiper, a short-billed and long-tailed species found in North American prairie grasslands.

Noisy male black-tailed godwit calling to his chicks in the Netherlands.

There are two species of turnstones, small, chunky birds with short, thick legs and a wedge-like, somewhat upturned bill, deployed to flick seaweed and small pebbles on the shore. The single species of ruff is unique, with adult breeding males having distinctive head tufts and neck plumes. Finally, the three species of phalaropes spend more time on water than any of the other shorebirds, and are often seen swimming and spinning, aided by their lobed toes.

If you do a tally of the sandpiper family's species you will see we are one short. As ever, when it comes to classifying birds there is endless debate about where some birds should be placed, and the shorebirds are no exception. The now-endangered Tuamotu sandpiper, of the Pacific islands of its name, is a small shorebird, with a short, slender bill and dark-brown, almost russet appearance. It is more closely related to the tattlers than the true sandpipers. Its late cousin, the white-winged sandpiper, discovered in 1773 during Captain Cook's voyage to the Polynesian Islands, became extinct sometime over the ensuing 100 years or so; today only one specimen exists.

The plovers and allies

The other major family, the plovers and allies (Charadriidae), has a quite different group of birds. There are two subfamilies, the largest of which (Charadriinae) comprises 67 species of **lapwings, 'true' plovers** and the **Magellanic plover**. These are small to medium-sized, compactly built birds, 5¾ to 12 in (15 to 30 cm) long, with a short bill, large eyes, a thick neck and short to medium-length legs. In contrast to the sandpipers, the plovers are visual feeders, with large eyes which are well adapted for the search for food. They tend to run in bursts, pausing periodically to scan the ground, and sometimes crouch before pecking.

The lapwings (of genus *Vanellus*) comprise 24 species. These are amazing birds, with their crests, wing-spurs or wattles, in 16 species, which are always more showy in the males. Lapwings occur worldwide, except in the arctic, and most are tropical and non-migratory. The origin of the word 'lapwing' tells us something about their wonderful display. 'Hleapewince' is the Old English term for the lapwing, derived from *hleapan* (leap) and *wincian* (to jerk). And that's just what lapwings do as they tumble, roll, twist and dive to herald the advent of spring.

The true plovers number 42 species: four species of tundra plovers (the grey, and three

On their tundra breeding grounds, these golden plovers are superbly camouflaged. Adult males are much darker than females – with more black on the face, throat and belly. In winter, males and females are indistinguishable, when their upper parts are brown-gray, the breast is grayish, and the belly is pale.

Compare the female American golden plover in its breeding plumage (above, in Alaska) with the juvenile plumage of the Pacific golden plover (below, in the Galapagos Islands).

*The unmistakable and elegant black-winged stilt. There are two subspecies,
both of which breed mainly by shallow freshwater lakes, marshes and swamps.*

golden plovers), and 38 small plover species. Most of these have slender wings, well adapted for long migratory flights. The tundra plovers breed mainly in arctic and northern regions. Their golden or gray spangled upper parts contrast superbly with black underparts, from face to belly.

The small plovers are tremendously varied in their distribution, habitats, and behavior. Most have varied head and breast-band markings, which play a part in displays, and help the bird blend with the background while sitting on the nest. Among the small plovers are the 32 members of the *Charadrius* genus, including two species of ringed plovers, six sand plovers, the Kentish plover and the killdeer. There are five species of dotterel among the shorebirds, and some argue that at least two of these belong to the *Charadrius* genus.

There is no argument about the strangest of all the true plovers, the wrybill, confined to New Zealand. Its sideways-bent bill is supremely adapted for extracting small prey from the undersides of stones in its riverbed nesting grounds in South Island.

Finally there is the enigmatic Magellanic plover, found in the southernmost reaches of South America. Not yet included in any DNA comparisons, it is debatable whether this turnstone-like bird is even a shorebird; in some ways it is more like a gull, and its pale gray and white plumage is quite unlike that of other shorebirds. It feeds its young by regurgitation, making use of its large crop for carrying food (as well as for displays, when puffed up), again more akin to the gulls.

The second subfamily within the Charadriidae is the Recurvirostrinae, containing **oystercatchers**, **avocets**, **stilts** and the rare **ibisbill** (living along high-mountain streams of Central Asia). The ten species of oystercatchers are widespread and distinctive, with their pied plumage, stocky appearance, thick orange bill, short pinkish legs, and red-orange eye rings. But there are variations on these generalized features: the American black, blackish, variable and sooty oystercatchers all have near pure-black plumages, which immediately raises questions in one's mind as to why some species are pied and others are not.

With their truly long, pink legs, straight bill, and, with the exception of one species, pied plumage, the five species of stilts are surely the most elegant of all birds – real waders — which tend to nest around saline lakes. The banded stilt, found only in Australia, nests in massive, dense colonies, sometimes consisting of more than a hundred thousand nests. These colonies are mainly found in desert regions, but only when the rains come, which can be as infrequently as only once every ten or more years. It is amazing to think that the first nest was not discovered until 1930!

The avocets (four species), with their delicate, upcurved bills and long legs, typically feed in water with a sideways sweeping action of the bill, but will regularly swim in water too deep for wading. The Andean avocet is unusual among the four avocet species in being found at high altitude, as opposed to near sea level on the coast; its relatively shorter legs and bulkier body are well adapted for local conditions.

The other shorebird families

In many ways similar to plovers, the stone curlews and thick-knees (the Burhinidae family) also occur mainly in the southern hemisphere, though the stone curlew breeds as far north as southern Britain. All nine species have large yellow eyes, long stout yellow or greenish legs, and knobbly knees, and are mainly nocturnal.

One of the most extraordinary families of birds, never mind shorebirds, comprises the eight species of jacanas (Jacanidae). With their long legs, and elongated toes and claws, these gems are supremely adapted for life on floating vegetation, and even brood and carry their young between their wings and body. But it is their mating and parental adaptations which have aroused most interest: females tend to be larger than males, and mate with several, leaving each to care for eggs and brood.

Next we have the two species of painted snipes (Rostratulidae). These birds look like exotic woodcocks and snipes, yet the DNA analysis points to a close ancestral relationship with the jacanas.

Two families of odd-looking shorebirds remain: one (Thinocoridae) containing the four species of seedsnipes of South America, and the other (Pedionomidae) with the

Stone curlew keeping a watchful eye on its brood.

Australian plains-wanderer. The seedsnipes are more like partridges, though their narrow wings render them shorebird-like.

Debatable shorebirds

Finally we are left with the group of birds which some say are shorebirds. The coursers, pratincoles and crab plover (Glareolidae) total 18 species. The amazing crab plover, with its huge black bill and habit of nesting in burrows, is well adapted to avoiding the heat of some of the hottest deserts in the world. Crab plovers are very closely related to the gulls, and whether they merit inclusion among the shore-birds is indeed debatable.

The pratincoles are very long-winged, tern-like shorebirds. They hunt for insects in the air, and nest in colonies. Coursers, as their name implies, run at speed on their long legs in predominantly arid habitats. One of the coursers, the Egyptian plover of central Africa, is the so-called 'crocodile-bird' refered to in the writings of the Greek historian Herodotus (c.485-425 BC), known as the Father of History. Well illustrated in ancient drawings within the pyramids, this plover has a chunky body, striking deep gray and black upper parts and orange-peach underparts. This really is an unusual bird, for it buries its eggs in the sand of riverbeds to protect them from the heat and from predators.

Some species, and indeed families, are clearly more shorebird-like than others. Table 1 on page 68 lists all the species of shorebirds (including three species now believed to be extinct), and gives a summary of their breeding ranges and mating systems. The debatable shorebirds are not listed because, in our view, these are more akin to gulls.

While the taxonomy of shorebirds will doubtless change in the years ahead, we have tried to provide an introduction to shorebirds as a whole. Already it is evident that we have a phenomenal variety of shapes, sizes, colors, and habits.

The crab plover – a debatable shorebird, which feeds heavily on crabs – on the Indian Ocean coast.

Appearance

Look at any shorebird, as millions of birdwatchers have done. What do you see? These, after all, are among the most challenging of birds to identify. Look at the overall shape of the bird: is it tall and slender, or small and dumpy? What about the bill, is it long, short, blunt, pointed, upturned or down-curved? What color is the bill, and is there a colored tip? What about the legs – are they long, short, thick or fine? Are they dark, yellow, orange, pink or red? And this is the easy part.

Plumage and molts

Now we come to plumage, which can tell us so much about the bird's age, sex, phases of life, and in some cases its geographical 'race' (there is great variation in some of the shorebirds, such as the dunlin). The key to recognizing the shorebird's appearance lies in knowing in which of the stages (typically six) of the plumage sequence the bird appears. Is it a downy chick, or a juvenile? Is it in its first non-breeding or breeding plumage, or in its adult (second/subsequent years') non-breeding or breeding plumage? Unusually, the three golden plover species, and a few other shorebirds, have a special 'eclipse' plumage, which occurs between breeding and non-breeding plumages; scattered amongst the black breast feathers are yellowish eclipse feathers, so distinctive in golden plovers, particularly during the chick-rearing period.

All feathers suffer from wear and tear, and abrade, thus losing their strength, and they need to be replaced. At particular times of the year the shorebird sheds each of its several thousand feathers during what is known as the 'molt' (derived from the Latin word *muto*, meaning change). During each molt phase feathers are shed and replaced, but gradually and in an ordered way. On different parts of the body, such as the tail or the outer wing, one feather will be shed every few days or so as the new one pushes through. This progression of feather loss is important; if a bird were to molt all its flight feathers at once, it would be flightless and would have to find the extra resources needed to produce new ones, while

American oystercatcher, which has distinctive yellow eyes, unlike the red-eyed Eurasian oystercatcher.

also being vulnerable to predators, and unable to fly in pursuit of its own food.

Of course, when you are out in the field, you have to make snap judgements. You are looking at those parts of the body where the feathers are so distinctive, yet variable: the primary (outer) and shorter secondary (inner) wing feathers, the remaining wing 'covert' feathers (both underwing and on top), the head, tail, breast, belly, scapular, mantle and rump feathers, and so on. On each of these areas the feathers wear with time, especially those more exposed to the rigors of wind turbulence in flight or to strong sun, which can bleach the colors. They are thus molted from the body at a certain time, which helps us identify the shorebird in detail.

Let's look closely at the changing appearance of the shorebird as it develops. The downy chick has grown into a fledged juvenile. It can fly, but there are tell-tale signs such as the odd tag of down fluttering on its head. Soon, though, its appearance is fresh and clean. After a few weeks, or even months, as more feathers are replaced, the non-breeding plumage is attained. Some of these birds will now be on their wintering grounds, but others may be resident year-round. Winter ensues and the feathers endure a lot of wear. Intriguingly, as spring approaches, marked changes occur in some species, and those which breed in their first year, as many do, don a breeding plumage. The belly, breast and face, in particular, become darker and more striking; pale underparts become blackish, brown, reddish, spotted or streaked. The mantle and scapulars become blotched or streaked, and darker. In the godwits, tundra plovers, knots, stints, and shanks, the breeding plumage is stunning; they become gorgeously imposing and attractive. In some of the larger shorebirds, such as the curlews and stilts, which do not breed in their first year, the same non-breeding plumage remains into the spring, though by now many of the feathers look worn.

By its second summer, the shorebird is an adult. Its appearance is clean, sharp and fresh; after all, the body feathers are new and richly pigmented, having replaced the old, pale, frazzled and torn ones. And so the pattern of molt continues, through the key seasons, though after its first year the older adult tends to attain its non-breeding plumage later in the summer.

Adaptations in size, shape and form
What do the size and shape of the bird, and its distinctive characteristics, tell us about, for

This northern lapwing chick is only a day or so old. Yet already it is fending for itself, feeding mainly on small insects on the mud surface. At the first sign of danger it will seek cover, while its parents mob any approaching predators.

example, the northern lapwing tugging at an earthworm in the ground, or the sturdily built curlew with its massive bill deep in the mud; the stout Eurasian oystercatcher hammering at a mussel with its long, thick bill, or the trim sanderling flashing by on its narrow, compact, pointed wings? Much of what we see in the size, shape and posture of these birds has been honed by nature on the non-breeding grounds, where there can be stiff competition for food.

The bill

One of the most striking features of shorebirds is their bill. Bill size and shape, more than any other external characteristics, represent adaptations to the species' food and feeding habitat. Plovers and stone curlews possess short, conical bills with a hard and pointed tip, ideal for catching prey such as worms or mollusks in the ground. Most of the scolopacids have fairly soft bills which are more or less elongated, curved, and with a sensitive tip which is often flexible too. These birds 'feel' for their prey by touch, or snatch them at or just below the water or muddy surface. The bill length of the far eastern curlew may measure 8 in (20 cm), and in the common snipe the bill can represent over a quarter of the total body length.

The legs

The legs tell us much about the habits of shorebirds. Most species have long legs, which are perfect for two purposes: wading in water, and running on a fairly smooth surface, such as a mountain heath, a sandy beach or desert. Functionally, the bird's foot is made up by the toes alone. The visible part of the leg, above the toes, consists of tarsus and tibia, and the joint between these, looking like a knee turned backwards, is actually the heel. Long legs, primarily geared for running, such as in plovers and thick-knees, are characterized by a long tarsus and a fairly short tibia. Shorebird species finely adapted to wading have a very long tibia, readily apparent in avocets and stilts.

Some shorebirds, such as the snipes and woodcocks, have short legs but very long toes.

The American avocet's upturned bill filters out food as it scythes through water.

These birds walk on wet, mossy vegetation and do not normally run, and wade only in very shallow water. Long toes have evolved to the extreme in jacanas, enabling them to walk on floating vegetation. The length of the middle toe equals 39 per cent of the body length in the African jacana, but only eight per cent in the Eurasian oystercatcher.

Phalaropes spend most of their life swimming – on freshwater pools in their breeding grounds, and on the oceans where they spend the non-breeding season. They do not possess the familiar webbed feet found in gulls or ducks. Rather, their toes have lobes or flaps (like the coots and grebes), which extend to provide propulsion as the foot is moved backwards in the water, and when moved forwards, the lobes fold along the toes to minimize water resistance.

The semipalmated plover has semi-webbed feet.

Of all the shorebirds, avocets come closest to having traditional webbed feed, but many of the scolopacids, as well as some of the plovers, possess semipalmate or semi-webbed feet – small skin membranes in the gaps between the toes. Although most shorebirds can swim if they have to, and some do so more than occasionally, the semi-webbed toes are more likely adapted to walking on mudflats.

Wings
Strong and pointed, the wings of most shorebirds are designed for speed. The curved profile of the innermost part of the wings provides a strong lift, yet being fairly short, the wings

Red-necked phalaropes spend much of their lives swimming.

create a minimum of drag. These features provide vital advantages, not only for long-distance migration, but also in coordinated high-speed flocking flights so typical of shorebirds when avoiding attacking raptors.

The woodcocks have rather rounded wings, which they use in an explosive vertical flight when disturbed. Rounded wingtips greatly enhance maneuverability – a great advantage among dense bushes and trees. A similar wing type is characteristic of forest-living passerines and hawks. A peculiarly rounded wing is found in the northern lapwing; males, in particular, have a very broad wingtip, much more so than the females. Over their territories males perform flight displays which involve dramatic aerobatic maneuvers, and which demonstrate their prowess in fending off predators.

Display and fighting adornments

Sexual selection is apparently involved in several body structures including wings, and also in the colors of some of the shorebirds. The most remarkable example is seen in the ruff. Males are much larger than females, and possess a collar of long, seemingly broad feathers around their neck, hence the species' name. The color patterns of the birds' ruffs are unique to individuals, although they can be grouped into categories. Crests and spurs found in some lapwing species are other features that are probably sexually selected.

Some shorebirds, especially lapwings, oystercatchers and shanks, possess bright legs and bills, which probably serve a signal function. Bare wattles found in tropical lapwings and jacanas may serve signal functions too, and may also help in keeping the birds cool through heat loss.

Some species of lapwings and jacanas possess a long thorn-like spur on each wing joint. They use these spurs in territorial fights, mainly as weapons of threat. Although formidable-looking – in the Chilean lapwing the wing spurs measure almost ¾ in (18 mm) – the spurs are never used against predators. After all, lapwings would not want to get entangled with a predator.

An adult northern lapwing.

Migration and Movements

The wind birds are strong, marvelous fliers, averaging greater distances
in their migrations than any other bird family on earth.

Peter Matthiessen, *The Shorebirds of North America* (1967)

While we often think of the northern breeding grounds of shorebirds as their 'home', this can be misleading. Many of these birds come to the north for the huge invertebrate food supplies to sustain their chicks. They are there for a matter of only a few months, and then head south for more temperate conditions. Some of the best breeding areas for shorebirds are, for much of the year, among the harshest parts of the globe. Imagine it: in late spring, after much of the snow has thawed, the birds arrive exhausted after a long haul; they have just three months to find a mate, rear a family, and survive the daily uncertainties of where predators will appear and where food will be most accessible. And then they have to leave, before conditions deteriorate. As most of the world's shorebirds breed on tundra, heaths and inland marshes of northern and temperate regions, they have to undertake enormously long migrations south to escape the rigors of winter, and then return north the following spring.

Why migrate?

This raises a fundamental question: how did migration evolve? We know from detailed scientific studies that tens of thousands of years ago much of the central and northern globe was gripped in ice – The Ice Age. For the shorebirds, and many other birds, this posed challenges – trying to find places to feed, to breed and to survive. In many areas there will have been competition for space and food and so movement was vital. And if chance encounters led to birds settling and doing well in particular parts in the north, which were

Huge dunlin flocks perform spectacular aerial maneuvers.

ice-free, then they will have returned to breed there again. You can see natural selection panning out: those birds which migrated between wintering and breeding areas most efficiently, and which produced most young, will have won a significant advantage over their peers. This is a crude simplification of what will have happened in evolutionary terms. But it is worth a thought when you look at migration maps for birds, or indeed other animals (not least nomadic tribes of people). But for shorebirds it is the sheer distance traveled which is amazing: just think of the American golden plover making non-stop 4350 mile (7000 km) flights twice each year between South America and the northern Canadian and Alaskan tundra.

It is in the non-breeding season that the majority of shorebirds live up to their name. Many nest close to water, or have affinities with wetlands. But in their wintering grounds they congregate on the coastal, muddy shores. Most probe and dig for food in soft substrates. Mudflats and soft beaches are therefore good places to feed. These habitats are not randomly distributed; most are found along the marine shorelines of the world, especially in estuaries and along shallow coastal waters strongly influenced by tidal waters. During low tide, the mudflats are exposed and a teeming supply of small invertebrates is available to the shorebirds.

The flyways

Shorebird migrations are concentrated into 'flyways' above the shorelines of the world. Although some species, such as several of the snipes and shanks, migrate inland along freshwater systems and some do not use wetlands at all (notably the Eurasian dotterel), most of the shorebirds migrate along the shoreline, which is their preferred habitat.

In North America during the fall, a large number of shorebirds quit their breeding grounds in arctic Canada for the Atlantic coast of Canada and the northern U.S.A., and from there proceed southwards. Some, like the American golden plover, cross the West Atlantic and make landfall on the northeastern shoulder of South America. Many shorebirds spend the winter there, but others continue south, along the coast or across the massive forest tracts, to reach wintering grounds in Argentina, Uruguay, and southern Brazil. Some, such as Hudsonian godwits and red knots, go all the way to Tierra del Fuego. Shorebirds also migrate south along the interior of North America to reach the Mexican

Flyways Used by Shorebirds on Migration

(Source: Wader Study Group)

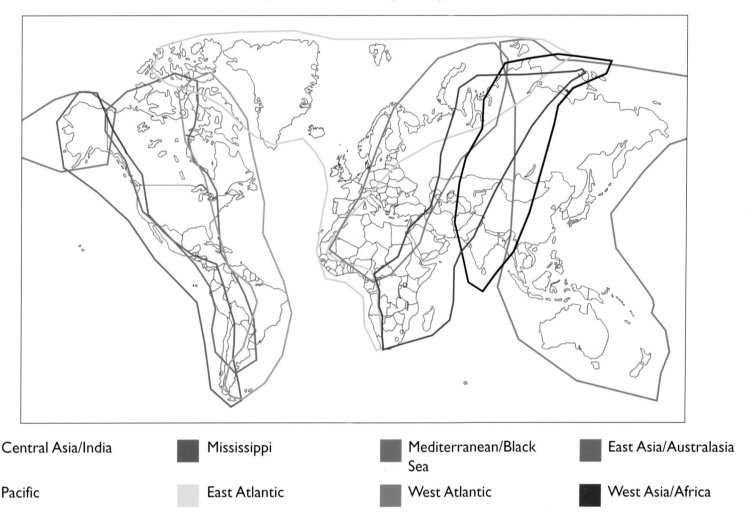

■ Central Asia/India　　■ Mississippi　　■ Mediterranean/Black Sea　　■ East Asia/Australasia

■ Pacific　　■ East Atlantic　　■ West Atlantic　　■ West Asia/Africa

Within each flyway, birds migrate between breeding, staging and wintering grounds along fairly consistent routes. However, the journeys south in late summer/autumn, and north in late winter/spring, can be along different routes. Each flyway is composed of a huge number of overlapping routes used by each species, and by the different populations of each of these. Birds travel along a wide range of routes from and to their breeding grounds, using sites and habitats best suited to their needs. International conservation efforts strive to protect flyway sites with major concentrations of each species. Some sites host more than 10 per cent of the flyway populations of given species, and therefore merit a very high priority for protection.

A juvenile dunlin in a characteristic roosting pose. There are nine
subspecies, each differing in size and color of upperparts in breeding plumage.

Gulf, and yet others take the flyway along the west coast.

The East Atlantic flyway along the coast of Europe and West Africa carries shorebirds from as wide an area as the eastern Canadian Arctic right across to north central Siberia. A flyway over the Mediterranean and Black Seas partly merges with this flyway, and continues down the interior of East Africa as well as to the coast of West Africa. Further important shorebird flyways go from North Siberia to India and along the coasts of East Asia to Southeast Asia, Australia and the Pacific islands.

Who uses these flyways? Intriguingly, there are frequently large differences in the migration patterns of different populations of the same species, and there are even differences between the sexes and different age groups within these. Grey plover females and juveniles tend to migrate to the tropics and subtropics, whereas adult males winter more in the temperate zone coasts, closer to their breeding grounds. Sharp-tailed sandpiper adults leave their Siberian breeding grounds and head straight for their Australian wintering grounds in a broadfront migration over land, whereas juveniles head for the northeast Asian coast, and then proceed southwards. Purple sandpipers show remarkable differences in wintering areas, and apparently do not move south to spend the winter along the shoreline nearest to their wintering grounds. Instead, while birds from Greenland spend the winter in Iceland, Icelandic birds move to the coasts of Labrador and Britain. Purple sandpipers breeding in southern Norway overwinter in Scotland, whereas those found on the Norwegian coast in winter are from northern Russia, and those breeding in Spitsbergen go all the way to southern Sweden.

Among shorebirds, the most common pattern of migration is for the northernmost species to travel farthest, with tropical and subtropical species being, as a rule, rather sedentary. Yet even the latter can undergo substantial movements. For instance, plovers breeding in Australia, and possibly also African lapwings, can move large distances in order to track suitable feeding conditions determined by the rain seasons; these are the 'rain migrants'.

The northward journey in spring and the southward journey in autumn can be quite different. Many species use different flyways during these periods, giving rise to the term 'loop migration'. Curlew sandpipers which have bred in western Siberia frequently migrate over the Baltic to reach the East Atlantic seaboard in autumn; yet in early spring they go northeast along the Mediterranean flyway, as along this route they can exploit the many wetlands of inland Russia. American golden plovers follow the West Atlantic flyway in autumn, yet choose the inland route over South America in spring. The use of different flyways may be linked to the distribution of suitable food resources in autumn and spring, but will also be due to different seasonal weather patterns which provide shorebirds with convenient tail winds for their migration.

Wintering flock of red knots in Florida.

Helping hands and neat tricks

Tail winds can strongly enhance shorebird migration. Their own propulsion gives shorebirds an air speed of only about 35 to 42 mph (60 to 70 kmph). They need to travel much faster than this though, so in order to ride on strong winds the flocks may rise to a height of several thousand feet. This is particularly important for those species which travel long distances without resting. Red knots, for instance, may cover the distance from their West African wintering grounds to their Siberian breeding grounds in just four or five 'hops', during which they have to stay airborne for a couple of days non-stop.

Such long flights demand huge amounts of energy. The birds prepare for migration by putting on copious amounts of fat. Compared to protein, fat provides eight to nine times more energy per volume. So, in several shorebird species, before the birds take off for a migration hop, almost 40 per cent of their body mass is fat. In order to feed efficiently, they have even developed large digestive tracts to help maximize energy production on a stopover site. As departure approaches they reabsorb parts of the tract and direct the protein from this to the flight muscles. Thus, the shorebirds are supremely prepared for their long journeys, but not

The northern lapwing has the broadest wings of all lapwings.
Most flocks on migration have 30 to 50 birds, though massive flocks occur. In winter, freezing weather
can cause these birds to migrate over large distances to temporary areas of sanctuary.

surprisingly on arrival at a stopover or wintering site they are frequently exhausted. They fall asleep as soon as they land and sometimes can be caught by hand.

Having finished breeding, northern shorebirds not only hurry to get away from inhospitable areas, but also start to renew their plumage. Although they have very strong flight feathers, these get very worn during the long flights, and need to be replaced annually. This is usually done after breeding, either on special molting grounds en route to their wintering grounds, or just after arrival.

The molting of feathers, winter survival, migration, and breeding are all energy-consuming events, and for those shorebirds on the move during March to May, and then from July to October, the time schedule is perilously tight. Those wintering on the northernmost wintering grounds face yet other difficulties. Bad weather may make their feeding grounds and food difficult to get at, and they may have to migrate out of the adverse areas in mid winter. This is often seen in northern lapwings wintering in Britain, which have to move south and west to seek milder climes; or they may go into a period of fasting, an option chosen by bar-tailed godwits on British estuaries during cold spells.

While shorebirds in the tropics face the uncertainties of the rains, which vary from year to year, and over longer episodes, in creating ideal wetland conditions for nesting, those in the north have seemingly impossible challenges: when to leave, how to feed up, where to stop off, and how to trade-off time needed for feather molts and long-distance flights. Yet, amazingly, many of these birds breed in and overwinter in traditional areas – often nesting in tundra or wintering in mudflat locations just a few feet away from where they were in previous years. Clearly, familiarity with these areas is vital to the survival of the birds. That they move between these areas, across the globe, unerringly arriving at the same spots year after year is surely one of the great marvels of the natural world.

And just consider this: a 22-year-old red knot, shot in Spain, had probably traveled twice each year, back and forth, between Siberia and South Africa, notching up 700,000 air miles in the process (the distance to the moon and back). That is simply astonishing!

Wintering flock of bar-tailed godwits roosting on saltmarsh.

Mating and Social Behavior

Shorebirds show a more bewildering variety of mating and social systems than any other group of birds. Although monogamy is the most common mating system in shorebirds, as in other birds, many show different variants of polygyny (where one male is mated to more than one female), polyandry (where one female is mated to more than one male) and a strange system usually referred to as 'double-clutching' (whereby a female produces one clutch for the male to incubate and then another clutch for herself to sit on). Around 20 per cent of shorebird species are polygamous, most of these being polygynous.

Typical breeding cycle

It is difficult to generalize on the breeding season of a shorebird, as this differs between species and regions. As a rule though, in most of the monogamous species the male returns to the breeding grounds in early spring. He displays to stake out his territory and after days, or even weeks, the female arrives. Now there is intense competition, with males singing in the air or on the ground to attract a female. Their aerial flight displays are fantastic. The plovers' performances usually involve jerky, stereotyped wing beats coupled with simple rhythmic songs of one or a few syllable notes. Many of the scolopacids display with wing vibrations whilst giving buzzing and croaking sounds. Some shanks perform gliding flights accompanied by loud whistles. The flight pattern and sounds appear to underline one another, providing a marvelous sense of rhythm and synchronization.

Once paired up, often with last year's mate, the male copulates with the female, especially around the time she ovulates – a few days before egg laying. Some birds copulate dozens or even scores of times over a week or so, and during this time males tend to guard their mates closely to avoid being 'cuckolded'. The nest is a small depression in the ground, and once the four eggs (typically) are laid, the male and female share incubation. The eggs are pear-shaped and fit snugly into the nest with the pointed ends facing inwards, as this

Mating American avocets; note the longer, straighter bill of the male.

helps to minimize heat loss. The eggs are striking; background colors vary from white, brown, buff, gray, green or red, and on these are blotches, streaks and spots which are brown, black or other dark colors. Invariably they are cryptic, and it can be extraordinarily difficult to see some clutches even a few feet away. Many females lay eggs with patterns that are unique to them – blueprints which vary little from year to year over their lifespan.

In monogamous species, males and females usually share incubation duties equally. Some birds will sit for shifts of 12 hours or longer, only leaving the nest when relieved by their partner. This goes on for about three weeks (longer in larger species) until the eggs hatch. Then there can be an almighty din as the excited parents lead their chicks from the nest, often after just a few hours. Now the parents have to protect their young from predators, and lead them to safe havens for feeding. Some species stay close to the nest vicinity, but others, such as northern greenshanks, run miles in a few days. The chicks are remarkably strong and fit. If they chill, as inevitably happens in tundra regions, they are brooded by their parents, but once they warm up they are off again – to feed.

The parents' routine is extraordinary: they are sentinel for predators, giving special warning calls to the chicks to hide or to lie still (chicks have superb camouflage), and fend off predators aggressively or with an array of distraction displays. Many shorebirds rely on camouflage and a surreptitious existence for their own and their nest's protection. If a predator comes too close to the nest or young, the parent will try to lead it away by pretending to have a broken wing, and crying as if hurt. In trying to be seen as an easier meal than their nest or chicks, the parent will also scuttle along the ground with ruffled feathers, giving mouse-like squeaks. Others, notably the larger species, determinedly attack predators which venture near nest or chicks. Eurasian curlews forcefully drive away ravens from their nesting territories, and grey plovers in the arctic do not hesitate to attack raptors as large as rough-legged buzzards. Aggressive shorebirds may even act as protective umbrellas to other, more timid birds, which often nest in their vicinity.

As the chicks mature they require less brooding, and then some broods amalgamate

Superbly camouflaged red knot on the nest in NE Greenland tundra.

loosely or even into crèches, notably in some of the curlews, little stint and least sandpiper. As the chicks fledge, after around four to five weeks, the adults leave (the female days or even weeks before the male) and shortly afterwards the fledglings also quit the nesting grounds. Only one or two fledglings tend to make it from the original clutch of four eggs, and less than half of these will survive the first year. Some studies suggest that siblings stick together on the southerly migration, and even on their wintering grounds, but it is very unlikely that they meet up with their parents in winter to form family parties, as some geese do.

All of this suggests that the breeding cycle goes to plan: invariably it does not. Many nests are depredated by foxes and crows, or even deserted due to severe weather. Some pairs will try to re-nest, but others will 'divorce', with the female moving further afield to secure another mate.

Great snipe males lekking; they leap in the air with tails fanned.

Variable mating systems

Polygamy often leads to family situations in which only one of the mates takes on the parental duties. A prerequisite for this may be that the young should be able to manage without much parental help. In shorebirds this is certainly the case. Only a few, such as common snipe, woodcocks and oystercatchers, bring food to their chicks.

Entirely single-parent care is found in polygynous shorebirds with a lek system. Two such well-studied species are the ruff and the great snipe. In these, females alone incubate and raise the chicks, whereas the males do little but compete for females! On the leks, the males gather in a fairly concentrated area where they keep small individual territories of only a few square feet, from which they announce their presence. Great snipes use song and the exposure of white-patterned tail feathers, whereas ruff display their gorgeous breast feathers in total silence. The pair bond in these species lasts no longer than the few seconds it takes to copulate.

Ruffs vary enormously in their breast-feather patterns, from white to rufous spotted and glossy black. Moreover, perhaps uniquely among birds, the patterns of the display feathers are linked to behavioral traits. Dark males are the ones holding the small display territories ('resident males'), whereas white males ('satellites') appear on the territories of the resident males, where they are tolerated. Possibly, their presence helps in attracting females, and although the most dominant of the resident males are the ones which obtain most copulations, the satellites which manage to keep close to the dominant ruffs obtain some copulations too.

A less extreme polygynous system is the so-called 'resource defense polygyny', a system found in northern lapwings and pectoral sandpipers. Here, males monopolize territorial resources, such as food and breeding grounds. The males holding the most resources are the winners in competition for females. They may attract two, three, or even four mates, while inferior males remain bachelors. In this contest, male quality is in itself one of the resources: the flight display aerobatics of the lapwing males appear to mimic the birds' individual ability to chase away predators – indeed, this is bound to be a valuable piece of information for females prospecting for a mate. A male pectoral sandpiper tries to impress a female by flying over her, inflating his chest sac while making loud hooting sounds as he passes. Although male pectoral sandpipers play no part in looking after the youngsters, male lapwings at least help one of their mates.

In polyandrous shorebirds, there are systems matching those found in the polygynous species, except that the sex roles are reversed. Females are the competitive sex in polyandrous shorebirds, tend to be brighter colored and/or larger than the males, and the males take on most or all of the parental duties. In the remarkable northern jacanas, females defend territories to which males are attracted; several males can take up territories within these, which they defend against other males.

Spotted sandpiper females try to monopolize several males on their territories simultaneously. Intriguingly, Lew Oring and colleagues, working on Little Pelican Island in Minnesota, have used DNA fingerprinting to show that some males pairing early in spring with females actually cuckold these females' later mates! It seems that females store sperm from early

Male ruffs fighting at a lek site. Typically, each male defends a patch around 3 ft (1 meter) from neighbors. Females (reeves) visit the lek and are mated by one or more males; tussles between males can involve pecking and kicking.

copulations, and that when some of these get second or third mates later in the season, and put them on eggs, the poor chaps are actually incubating and raising offspring of the first male that mated with the female in early spring! In other species, notably phalaropes and the Eurasian dotterels, females attempt to mate with several males in succession. Having laid one clutch for a male to sit on, they search for the next mate. This can take the females great distances: some female dotterels can have mates in both Scotland and Norway in the same year.

Double-clutching is found in three arctic and subarctic scolopacids (Temminck's and little stints, and sanderling) and in the mountain plover. In this system, a female lays one clutch of eggs for a male to look after, and then a second clutch, fathered by the same or a different male, which she looks after.

More polyandrous and double-clutching species belong to shorebirds than to all other bird taxa combined. Why? This is one of the hardest questions to answer. Long distances between breeding and wintering grounds, differences in sex ratios on the nesting grounds, the fact that one bird only may be needed to care for a clutch of eggs have all been suggested as contributory factors. Recently, comparative studies have suggested that male-only parental care tends to be more prevalent in bird families (in taxonomic terms) that nest at low density, possibly because the risks of deserting eggs or chicks to find other matings are that much lower.

Lifetime production

We still know very little about the overall productivity of shorebirds. The work on spotted sandpipers indicates that, over a bird's lifetime (of up to nine years), females produce around five fledglings and males produce three to four. In the common sandpiper, females produce around three to four fledglings in a lifetime. As in most birds, a minority of individuals produce a disproportionate number of fledglings. In many species it may well be the case that 15 to 20 per cent of individuals produce more than half the fledglings in a population.

How long do shorebirds live? Most species have some adults that have lived to over ten years old. The oystercatchers live well into their twenties and even thirties; some of the Eurasian and African black oystercatchers do not breed until three or four years old and one was recorded as having bred for the first time aged 14.

Year in the Lives of Shorebirds

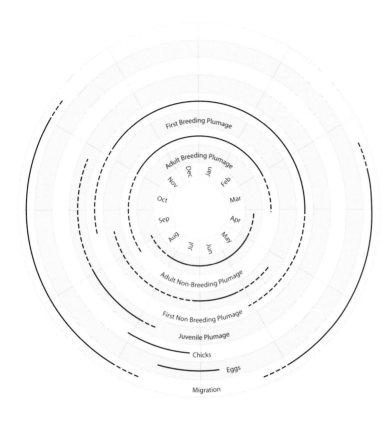

Red Knot (left)
Note how tightly squeezed the knot is in laying eggs and rearing chicks over a period of only 6-8 weeks during June-July in its far north arctic breeding grounds.

Eurasian Dotterel (right)
Nesting further south, on mountain plateaux, the breeding grounds are available to the birds from late May through to late August. In the north, though, where snow lies later in spring, they may start egg laying into late June. Females can lay several clutches, each incubated by separate males, and some may travel further north each time after they put a male down on eggs.

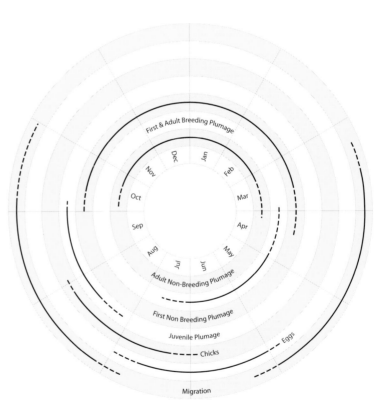

Each diagram shows periods of migration, egg laying, chick rearing, and development of plumages of juvenile, first year non-breeding, first year breeding, adult non-breeding and adult breeding phases of life.

Redshank (left)
Nesting in a variety of coastal and inland wetlands across the Palaearctic, redshanks can nest in early April in the south, though begin nesting as late as July in the far north.

Blacksmith Lapwing (right)
Nesting in southern African wetlands, this bird is mainly sedentary. There is no nesting season; they tend to nest at the start of dry seasons. In any year they will produce two broods. Flooding and predation are the main causes of chick losses.

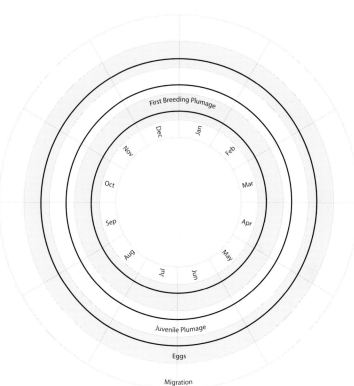

Food and Feeding

Shorebirds, like rats, crows, men, and other widespread and prosperous creatures, are euryphagous – partial, that is, to a variety of plant and animal food.

Peter Mathiessen, *The Shorebirds of North America* (1967)

Shorebirds feed primarily on invertebrate prey, but in some species a surprisingly high proportion of the diet consists of plant matter, notably berries. Plovers living on tundra and montane habitats are particularly prone to taking berries. Arriving there to find more or less snow-covered breeding grounds in spring, Eurasian golden plovers feed largely on crowberries, which have remained fresh and frozen in the snow since the previous fall. These berries form on plants growing on the drier ridges, and they are among the first signs of plant life to emerge above the snow in spring. The plovers gain rich supplies of carbohydrates from these berries to sustain them while they await the late spring thaw and greater access to food. Crowberries are popular food for golden plovers and several species of curlew well into late summer, and even during fall migration. Eskimo curlews, now almost extinct, were known to feed so extensively on crowberries before leaving Labrador that their plumage got blue-stained!

Of all the shorebirds, the seedsnipes are closest to vegetarians. These birds have an appearance and lifestyle more like grouse and partridges, yet have almost finch-like bills, and a basic food supply of buds, shoots, bits of leaves and seeds. Most shorebirds, however, do not feed to any great degree on vegetative matter. Instead, most feed on adult and larval insects on their breeding grounds.

Insects and worms: masses of food

In the Arctic, the huge production of insects provides the sustenance for the large shorebird populations there. Indeed, the phenomenal densities of insects may be one of the most

Bar-tailed godwit foraging; females have much longer bills than males for probing deeper in the mud.

important reasons for shorebirds finding these extreme northern areas so attractive. The larvae of midges and mosquitoes abound in the marshes and wetlands, and large cranefly larvae reside in the mossy ground. Other insects, notably beetles of various kinds, are also important. Where available in the soil, earthworms are very popular food items for many shorebirds. These worms are relatively large prey, and nutritionally extremely valuable.

Whereas plovers dig with their bills in order to get at the larvae just under the surface of the ground or vegetation, the long bills of scolopacids are equipped with numerous sensory cells so that the birds can find their prey by touch. Moreover, they can open the tip of the bill without opening the rest of it, a phenomenon known as rhynchokinesis. This enables the scolopacids to grab prey animals and swallow them with the aid of tongue movements, without having to remove the bill from the substrate – a great advantage when the bird has hit a dense clump of subterranean larvae.

The chicks hatch with relatively short beaks and are thus well adapted to feed on surface-active insects. On the tundra, the chicks hatch when there is a myriad of adult insects; clouds of midges and mosquitoes abound, and the chicks run around pecking at tiny insects on or just above the near-frozen tundra or peat.

Interestingly, the food of males and females often differs, particularly in the long-billed scolopacids, such as the bar-tailed godwit. During the days needed for egg formation, females have to feed hard to amass the necessary energy and nutrients. Godwit females probe for food in the marshes, concentrating hard on their feeding, with their bill working like a sewing machine in soft, mossy substrates. Meanwhile, their mates, who have much shorter bills, stay vigilant, only pecking occasionally at food items mainly on the ground surface. A similar division of labor is found in many shorebirds, and in the sandpipers, snipes and allies a shorter bill in males than in females is the rule.

Specialist feeding methods

Some shorebirds have very specialized modes of feeding. Avocets sweep their long upturned

American oystercatcher chick. The legs and bill are strong after just a few days.

56

bills back and forth while wading in shallow water, thus capturing small aquatic organisms on the move. Stilts and phalaropes, with their fine bills, exploit the water's surface tension to capture small water droplets containing tiny prey animals: as the bill is gradually opened, the droplet 'wanders' up the bill, and the prey is then ingested.

As shorebirds move from inland terrestrial and aquatic habitats, where they breed, to a salty, mainly coastal habitat in the non-breeding season, their food changes dramatically. Now they feed on mollusks such as small snails and bivalves, and on small crustaceans and polychaete worms – all living on, or in, the mud and other sediments. This poses a new problem for the shorebird: salt balance. In their brackish and marine habitats shorebirds take in a surplus of sodium chloride, which is more than their kidneys can cope with. Fortunately, they possess special salt glands to deal with this problem. These are situated above each eye, in a shallow depression in the skull, and drain salty water to the nasal cavity where it is excreted through the nostrils to finally drip from the tip of the bill.

Typically tight flock of black-tailed godwits.

Shorebirds have a constantly running nose! Similar glands are found in all birds living in marine environments. When shorebirds are on their breeding grounds in non-salty habitats, most of their salt glands atrophy, as they are not needed and it would probably take a good deal of energy to keep them functional. But as soon as the birds start feeding on marine organisms again, their salt glands grow quickly and start to function.

There has been a huge shrinkage of the world's mudflats in recent decades, and those that remain are under considerable threat from human development. This has presented shorebirds with real problems. For some, like the Eurasian oystercatcher and Eurasian curlew, earthworms are an alternative prey to mudflat invertebrates, but many fields with

Juvenile Eurasian curlew clasping one of around a quarter million worms it will consume in its lifetime.

earthworms are frozen in winter. Nevertheless, increasing use is being made of grassland habitats, not least parks and fields, by the longer-billed shorebirds. And in curlews, there is even an interesting difference in habitat use between the sexes. Females, with their longer bills, are more likely to stick to the mudflats, while the shorter-billed males feed mainly on land in pastures and fields. Farmland is a more typical non-breeding habitat for Eurasian golden plovers and northern lapwings. Often flocks of these birds are exploited by piratical (kleptoparasitic) black-headed and common gulls. The gull sits close by, watching a food-searching plover, and as an earthworm is pulled up, the gull swiftly flies in to steal it. In such situations the plovers have been found to switch from large and energetically profitable worms to smaller items which can be handled so quickly that the chances are they can be swallowed before the gulls are able to snatch them.

Some shorebirds are even predators on other birds' chicks and eggs. Stone curlews and other curlews are known to feed in this way. One shorebird, the bristle-thighed curlew, regularly feeds on eggs of seabirds while wintering on the Pacific islands. It steals eggs from terns breeding in the Austral summer and it has a special technique of cracking the eggs by using a pebble, which it swings against the egg by the tip of its bill.

Another notorious egg-eater is the ruddy turnstone. This amazing bird frequently breeds in colonies of arctic terns (which loudly and aggressively protect their territories from all predators). The ruddy turnstone exploits this 'protective umbrella', by stealing and devouring tern eggs. This bird has a huge dietary range, and on one occasion a flock of ruddy turnstones was seen feeding on a rotting human corpse which drifted ashore on the beach. In some ways this is not so surprising; in early spring they have returned after a long, arduous journey, and need to build up reserves of calcium to form the eggshell. Hence the females, in particular, of several northern shorebird species have been observed feeding on fish and other small vertebrates such as lemmings in order to derive calcium from their bones. Not so long ago one of us saw a common sandpiper feeding on a dead sheep just hours after it had arrived on its nesting grounds from central Africa.

Long-billed dowitcher about to grab its prey deep in the mud.

Conservation

What do shorebirds and dinosaurs have in common? A crisis of environmental deterioration. Not since that fateful catastrophe 65 million years ago, when a large meteor hit our planet, has there been such a major period of animal extinction – not, that is, until recent decades.

Some scientists argue that the impact of that meteor hitting Earth was so massive that the ensuing debris clouded the atmosphere, giving rise to dark, cold conditions which saw out the dinosaurs. During various periods between then and now there have been comparable losses of animals and plants due to habitat loss, hunting, disturbance and pollution. Whole continents have lost much of their natural forests, plains and coastline, and thousands of species have been wiped out in mere seconds of their evolutionary existence on land or in the sea. Shorebirds are no exception to this, and over recent centuries have experienced remorseless losses of their wetland habitats, and severe hunting pressures.

Think of the young shorebird leaving its birth place in the far north; it takes off, having at last been deserted by its parents. In all probability, the fledgling will already have coped with predators, cold and wet weather, and food shortage. Perhaps it has already been on the coast feeding up for its journey. Something triggers the beginning of an amazing journey, and the youngster is off. What lies ahead? Will the traditional 'stepping-stone' areas be undisturbed, will there be sufficient food during the short time our delicate wader lands to feed frantically, will there be yet more predators about? And what about competition for food and shelter: where should the youngster land, and for how long?

Essentially, pressures on shorebirds fall under three categories: loss of habitats used in the non-breeding and breeding seasons; hunting, predation and disturbance; and changes in the environment as a whole, such as global warming, which impact on food availability as well as some of the rudiments of the life cycle of the birds themselves.

A ringed plover, alone in a barren waste of tundra in Russia, settling on its clutch of three eggs.

Habitat losses

Coastal wetlands have shrunk throughout the world. Even in the more developed countries, such as Britain, up to 90 per cent of some estuaries have been developed largely for industry, agriculture and housing. The ensuing contraction of mudflats has imposed a tight squeeze on space available to over-wintering shorebirds. For us, though, the greatest shock has been the statistics on losses of mudflats and other coastal habitats along the East Asian-Australasian flyway. Here, along the coasts of the Philippines, Indonesia, China, Taiwan, Korea and Japan, up to 70 per cent of habitats used by shorebirds stopping off on migration have been lost in the past 20 years. Think of the birds as they fly south searching out vital patches where they can bolster their reserves on the long journey. If the tidal flats are gone the birds risk starvation or exhaustion. Many hundreds of thousands of shorebirds must have perished because of this. In South Korea alone, the government proposes to 'reclaim' almost a million acres (half a million hectares) of mudflat, including over 150 estuaries. This could be catastrophic for some shorebird species.

The changes in agricultural practices throughout the world are also giving rise to losses of grassland and steppe habitats. Pastureland, in particular, has declined rapidly, affecting breeding and non-breeding populations. Then there is the problem of pesticide applications and pollution, which reduce the invertebrate food supplies. Disturbance from people, notably on beaches, and hunting are additional problems.

Hunting

When we look at some of the shorebirds themselves we begin to appreciate the crisis they face. One of the classic cases is the Eskimo curlew. Once an abundant bird in northern Canada, it was almost exterminated through being shot on migration, mainly over the U.S.A. In 1926 it was declared extinct, but in 1945 two birds were found in Texas, and today there may be as many as 20 birds. Yet back in the early twentieth century there are descriptions of huge flocks. E.H. Forbush mentioned in his classic tome *Game Birds, Wildfowl and Shorebirds* (1912) that Eskimo curlews and golden plovers appeared in such massive flocks that they appeared to 'almost darken the sun'. The American golden plovers were equally harried, with almost fifty thousand killed in one day. Now, both golden plover species are protected in the American continent.

Extinctions and threatened species

Recently, Theunis Piersma and colleagues based in the Netherlands produced a valuable overview of the conservation status of some of the shorebirds. We have added to this by listing all endangered shorebird species (Table 2, page 71). Three species have gone extinct, and the black stilt will possibly become extinct soon. The Eskimo curlew and the south-west Siberian-nesting slender-billed curlew are teetering on extinction, the latter due to hunting and probably losses of its Mediterranean wintering grounds. In fact, the slender-billed curlew is now Europe's rarest bird; no breeding record exists since the last record, timed some time between 1914 and 1924.

Black-tailed godwits, dunlin and others foraging in Poole Harbour, UK.

Nordmann's greenshank of eastern Russia is endangered for broadly similar reasons, and probably numbers fewer than a thousand birds. Some species have declined rapidly in recent years: the sociable lapwing, spoon-billed sandpiper and black-banded plover, for instance, may soon be endangered. And for some of the populations of the world's smallest islands, predator introductions are invariably cited as culprits. In all, around 40 species, almost a quarter of the world's shorebirds, are declining or at risk.

Global changes

Today, global warming, desertification and coastal habitat loss are the most significant threats. The former is the big unknown, though scientific predictions seem to agree that by the end of this century the climate may be up to 8°F (4°C) warmer. It is predicted that the largest effects on habitats will occur on the arctic tundra-breeding grounds presently used by millions of shorebirds. The extent of tundra is bound to contract, and sea-level rise will overwhelm many of the existing tidal flats throughout the world.

But it is not all gloom. There is terrific international cooperation in surveying and monitoring these birds. Important African-Eurasian and Asian-Pacific flyway protection strategies have been developed. The African-Eurasian governments' Flyway Conservation Treaty is now being implemented. Global networks of protected sites have been established. In the western hemisphere there is the real prospect of protecting almost 30 million shorebirds through the conservation and management of over 3 million acres (1.5 million hectares) of wetlands. And there are plans, and indeed actions, under way to recreate the equivalent of some of the mudflats already lost to sea-level rise. It remains an open question, however, as to whether these laudable actions are sufficient to reverse the negative impacts and trends.

All this is a far cry from where we started out – in the field marveling at the beauty, diversity and behavior of shorebirds. Still, it is a huge consolation that the sheer enjoyment of watching these birds motivates so many people to join forces to study and care for shorebirds and their habitats.

Table 1: Shorebird Species of the World (199 species)

English name	Latin name	Breeding region	Mating system
Family-Jacanidae			
African Jacana	*Actophilornis africanus*	Af	Pa
Madagascar Jacana	*Actophilornis albinucha*	Af	–
Lesser Jacana	*Microparra capensis*	Af	Mo
Comb-crested Jacana	*Irediparra gallinacea*	As, Au	Pa
Pheasant-tailed Jacana	*Hydrophasianus chirurgus*	As	Pa
Bronze-winged Jacana	*Metopidius indicus*	As	Pa
Northern Jacana	*Jacana spinosa*	CA	Pa
Wattled Jacana	*Jacana jacana*	SA	Pa
Family-Rostratulidae			
Painted Snipe	*Rostratula benghalensis*	Af, As, Au	Pa
South American Painted Snipe	*Rostratula semicollaris*	SA	Mo
Family-Thinocoridae			
Rufous-bellied Seedsnipe	*Attagis gayi*	SA	Mo
White-bellied Seedsnipe	*Attagis malouinus*	SA	–
Grey-breasted Seedsnipe	*Thinocorus orbignyianus*	SA	–
Least Seedsnipe	*Thinocorus rumicivorus*	SA	Mo
Family-Pedionomidae			
Plains-wanderer	*Pedionomus torquatus*	Au	Pa
Family-Scolopacidae			
Eurasian Woodcock	*Scolopax rusticola*	Eu, As	Pg
Amami Woodcock	*Scolopax mira*	As	–
Rufous Woodcock	*Scolopax saturata*	As	–
Sulawesi Woodcock	*Scolopax celebensis*	As	–
Moluccan Woodcock	*Scolopax rochussenii*	As	–
American Woodcock	*Scolopax minor*	NA	Pg
Solitary Snipe	*Gallinago solitaria*	As	–
Latham's Snipe	*Gallinago hardwickiii*	As	Mo
Wood Snipe	*Gallinago nemoricola*	As	–
Pintail Snipe	*Gallinago stenura*	As	Mo
Swinhoe's Snipe	*Gallinago megala*	As	Mo
Great Snipe	*Gallinago media*	Eu, As	Pg
Common Snipe	*Gallinago gallinago*	NA, Eu, As	Mo
African Snipe	*Gallinago nigripennis*	Af	Mo
Madagascar Snipe	*Gallinago macrodactyla*	Af	–
South American Snipe	*Gallinago paraguaiae*	SA	–
Puna Snipe	*Gallinago andina*	SA	–
Noble Snipe	*Gallinago nobilis*	SA	–
Giant Snipe	*Gallinago undulata*	SA	–
Andean Snipe	*Gallinago jamesoni*	SA	–

English name	Latin name	Breeding region	Mating system
Fuegian Snipe	*Gallinago stricklandii*	SA	–
Imperial Snipe	*Gallinago imperialis*	SA	–
Jack Snipe	*Lymnocryptes minimus*	Eu, As	Mo
Chatham Snipe	*Coenocorypha pusilla*	Oc	Mo
Subantarctic Snipe	*Coenocorypha aucklandica*	Oc	Mo (Pg)
Black-tailed Godwit	*Limosa limosa*	Eu, As	Mo
Hudsonian Godwit	*Limosa haemastica*	NA	Mo
Bar-tailed Godwit	*Limosa lapponica*	Eu, As	Mo
Marbled Godwit	*Limosa fedoa*	NA	Mo
Little Curlew	*Numenius minutus*	As	Mo
Eskimo Curlew	*Numenius borealis*	NA	–
Whimbrel	*Numenius phaeopus*	NA, Eu, As	Mo
Bristle-thighed Curlew	*Numenius tahitiensis*	NA	Mo
Slender-billed Curlew	*Numenius tenuirostris*	As	–
Eurasian Curlew	*Numenius arquata*	Eu, As	Mo
Long-billed Curlew	*Numenius americanus*	NA	Mo
Far Eastern Curlew	*Numenius madagascariensis*	As	–
Upland Sandpiper	*Bartramia longicauda*	NA	Mo
Spotted Redshank	*Tringa erythropus*	Eu, As	Mo (Pa)
Common Redshank	*Tringa totanus*	Eu, As	Mo
Marsh Sandpiper	*Tringa stagnatilis*	Eu, As	Mo
Common Greenshank	*Tringa nebularia*	Eu, As	Mo
Nordmann's Greenshank	*Tringa guttifer*	As	Mo
Greater Yellowlegs	*Tringa melanoleuca*	NA	–
Lesser Yellowlegs	*Tringa flavipes*	NA	Mo
Solitary Sandpiper	*Tringa solitaria*	NA	Mo
Green Sandpiper	*Tringa ochropus*	Eu, As	Mo
Wood Sandpiper	*Tringa glareola*	Eu, As	Mo
Terek's Sandpiper	*Tringa cinerea* (*Xenus cinereus*)	Eu, As	–
Common Sandpiper	*Actitis hypoleucos* (*Tringa hygoleucos*)	Eu, As	Mo
Spotted Sandpiper	*Actitis macularia* (*Tringa macularia*)	NA	Pa
Grey-tailed Tattler	*Heteroscelus brevipes* (*Tringa brevipes*)	As	Mo
Wandering Tattler	*Heteroscelus incana* (*Tringa incana*)	As, NA	Mo
Willet	*Catoptrophorus semipalmatus*	NA	Mo
Tuamotu Sandpiper	*Prosobonia cancellata*	Oc	–
White-winged Sandpiper	*Prosobonia leucoptera* (extinct)	Oc / NA, Eu, As	–
Ruddy Turnstone	*Arenaria interpres*		Mo
Black Turnstone	*Arenaria melanocephala*	NA	–

The breeding region is given for each as Eu = Europe (including Greenland), Af = Africa, As = Asia, Au = Australia, Oc = Oceania, NA = North America, SA = South America, and CA = Central America.

Mating system is given for each as Mo = monogamy (recorded/suspected), Pg = polygyny, Pa = Polyandry, Dc = double-clutching, – = no information

English name	Latin name	Breeding region	Mating system	English name	Latin name	Breeding region	Mating system
Short-billed Dowitcher	*Limnodromus griseus*	NA, As	Mo	Canarian Black Oystercatcher	*Haematopus meadewaldoi* (extinct)	Af	—
Long-billed Dowitcher	*Limnodromus scolopaceus*	NA	Mo	African Black Oystercatcher	*Haematopus moquini*	Af	Mo
Asian Dowitcher	*Limnodromus semipalmatus*	As	Mo	American Black Oystercatcher	*Haematopus bachmani*	NA	Mo
Surfbird	*Aphriza virgata*	NA	Mo	American Oystercatcher	*Haematopus palliatus*	NA, CA, SA	Mo
Great Knot	*Calidris tenuirostris*	As	Mo	Pied Oystercatcher	*Haematopus longirostris*	Au, Oc	Mo
Red Knot	*Calidris canutus*	NA, Eu, As	Mo	Variable Oystercatcher	*Haematopus unicolor*	Oc	Mo
Sanderling	*Calidris alba*	Na, Eu, As	Mo, Dc	Sooty Oystercatcher	*Haematopus fuliginosus*	As	Mo
Semipalmated Sandpiper	*Calidris pusilla*	NA	Mo	Blackish Oystercatcher	*Haematopus ater*	SA	Mo
Western Sandpiper	*Calidris mauri*	As, NA	Mo	Magellanic Oystercatcher	*Haematopus leucopodus*	SA	Mo
Little Stint	*Calidris minuta*	Eu, As	Dc	Ibisbill	*Ibidorhyncha struthersii*	As	Mo
Red-necked Stint	*Calidris ruficollis*	As	Mo	Black-winged Stilt	*Himantopus himantopus*	Eu, Af, As	Mo
Temminck's Stint	*Calidris temminckii*	Eu, As	Dc	White-headed Stilt	*Himantopus leucocephalus*	As, Au, Oc	Mo
Long-toed Stint	*Calidris subminuta*	As	Mo	Black Stilt	*Himantopus novaezelandiae*	Oc	Mo
Least Sandpiper	*Calidris minutilla*	NA	Mo	Black-necked Stilt	*Himantopus mexicanus*	NA, CA, SA, Oc	Mo
White-rumped Sandpiper	*Calidris fuscicollis*	NA	Pg	White-backed Stilt	*Himantopus melanurus*	SA	Mo
Baird's Sandpiper	*Calidris bairdii*	As, NA	Mo	Pied Avocet	*Recurvirostra avosetta*	Af, Eu, As	Mo
Pectoral Sandpiper	*Calidris melanotos*	As, NA	Pg	American Avocet	*Recurvirostra americana*	NA	Mo
Sharp-tailed Sandpiper	*Calidris acuminata*	As	Pg	Red-necked Avocet	*Recurvirostra novaehollandiae*	As	Mo
Purple Sandpiper	*Calidris maritima*	NA, Eu	Mo	Andean Avocet	*Recurvirostra andina*	SA	—
Rock Sandpiper	*Calidris ptilocnemis*	As, NA	Mo	Eurasian Golden Plover	*Pluvialis apricaria*	Eu, As	Mo
Dunlin	*Calidris alpina*	NA, Eu, As	Mo	Pacific Golden Plover	*Pluvialis fulva*	As, NA	Mo
Curlew Sandpiper	*Calidris ferruginea*	As, Na	Pg	American Golden Plover	*Pluvialis dominica*	NA	Mo
Stilt Sandpiper	*Micropalama himantopus*	NA	Mo	Grey Plover	*Pluvialis squatarola*	NA, Eu, As	Mo
Buff-breasted Sandpiper	*Tryngites subruficollis*	As, NA	Pg	Red-breasted Plover	*Charadrius obscurus*	Oc	Mo
Spoon-billed Sandpiper	*Eurynorhynchus pygmaeus*	As	Mo	Common Ringed Plover	*Charadrius hiaticula*	NA, Eu, As	Mo
Broad-billed Sandpiper	*Limicola falcinellus*	Eu, As	Mo	Semipalmated Plover	*Charadrius semipalmatus*	NA	Mo
Ruff	*Philomachus pugnax*	Eu, As	Pg	Long-billed Plover	*Charadrius placidus*	As	—
Wilson's Phalarope	*Phalaropus tricolor* (*Steganopus tricolor*)	NA	Pa	Little Ringed Plover	*Charadrius dubius*	Eu, As	Mo
Red-necked Phalarope	*Phalaropus lobatus*	NA, Eu, As	Pa	Wilson's Plover	*Charadrius wilsonia*	NA, SA	Mo
Red Phalarope	*Phalaropus fulicaria*	NA, Eu, As	Pa	Killdeer	*Charadrius vociferus*	NA, SA	Mo
				Black-banded Plover	*Charadrius thoracicus*	Af	Mo
Family-Burhinidae				St Helena Plover	*Charadrius sanctaehelenae*	Af	Mo
Stone-curlew	*Burhinus oedicnemus*	Eu, Af, As	Mo	Kittlitz's Plover	*Charadrius pecuarius*	Af	Mo
Senegal Thick-knee	*Burhinus senegalensis*	Af	Mo	Three-banded Plover	*Charadrius tricollaris*	Af	Mo
Water Dikkop	*Burhinus vermicularis*	Af	Mo	Forbes Plover	*Charadrius forbesi*	Af	Mo
Spotted Dikkop	*Burhinus capensis*	Af	Mo	Piping Plover	*Charadrius melodus*	NA	Mo (Pa)
Double-striped Thick-knee	*Burhinus bistriatus*	CA, SA	Mo	Chestnut-banded Plover	*Charadrius pallidus*	Af	Mo
Peruvian Thick-knee	*Burhinus superciliaris*	SA	—	Kentish Plover	*Charadrius alexandrinus*	NA, Eu, As, Af	Mo (Pa, Pg)
Bush Thick-knee	*Burhinus grallarius*	Au	Mo	White-fronted Plover	*Charadrius marginatus*	Af	Mo
Great Thick-knee	*Burhinus recurvirostris*	As	Mo	Red-capped Plover	*Charadrius ruficapillus*	Au	Mo
Beach Thick-knee	*Burhinus giganteus* (*Esacus magnirostris*)	Au, Oc	Mo	Malaysian Plover	*Charadrius peronii*	As	—
Family-Charadriidae				Javan Plover	*Charadrius javanicus*	As	—
Eurasian Oystercatcher	*Haematopus ostralegus*	Eu, As	Mo				

English name	Latin name	Breeding region	Mating system	English name	Latin name	Breeding region	Mating system
Collared Plover	*Charadrius collaris*	NA, SA	–	Javanese Wattled Lapwing	*Vanellus macropterus (extinct)*	As	–
Double-banded Plover	*Charadrius bicinctus*	Oc	Mo	Masked Lapwing	*Vanellus miles*	Au, Oc	Mo
Puna Plover	*Charadrius alticola*	SA	–	Blacksmith Plover	*Vanellus armatus*	Af	Mo
Two-banded Plover	*Charadrius falklandicus*	SA	–	Spur-winged Plover	*Vanellus spinosus*	Af, As, Eu	Mo
Lesser Sandplover	*Charadrius mongolus*	As	Mo	River Lapwing	*Vanellus duvaucelli*	As	–
Greater Sandplover	*Charadrius leschenaultii*	As	Mo	Black-headed Lapwing	*Vanellus tectus*	Af	Mo
Caspian Plover	*Charadrius asiaticus*	As	Mo	Spot-breasted Lapwing	*Vanellus melanocephalus*	Af	–
Oriental Plover	*Charadrius veredus*	As	–	Grey-headed Lapwing	*Vanellus cinereus*	As	Mo
Mountain Plover	*Charadrius montanus*	NA	Mo, Dc	Red-wattled Lapwing	*Vanellus indicus*	As	Mo
Rufous-chested Dotterel	*Charadrius modestus*	SA	Mo	White-headed Lapwing	*Vanellus albiceps*	Af	Mo
Hooded Plover	*Charadrius rubricollis*	Au	Mo	African Wattled Lapwing	*Vanellus senegallus*	Af	Mo
Shore Plover	*Charadrius novaeseelandiae*	Oc	Mo	Lesser Black-winged Lapwing	*Vanellus lugubris*	Af	Mo
Eurasian Dotterel	*Charadrius morinellus*	Eu, As	Pa	Greater Black-winged Lapwing	*Vanellus melanopterus*	Af	Mo
Red-kneed Dotterel	*Erythrogonys cinctus*	Au	Mo				
Tawny-throated Dotterel	*Oreopholus ruficollis*	SA	–	Crowned Lapwing	*Vanellus coronatus*	Af	Mo
Wrybill	*Anarhynchus frontalis*	Oc	Mo	Brown-chested Lapwing	*Vanellus superciliosus*	Af	Mo
Diademed Plover	*Phegornis mitchellii*	SA	–	Sociable Lapwing	*Vanellus gregarius*	Eu, As	Mo
Inland Dotterel	*Peltohyas australis*	Au	Mo	White-tailed Lapwing	*Vanellus leucurus*	Eu, As	Mo
Magellanic Plover	*Pluvianellus socialis*	SA	Mo	Pied Lapwing	*Vanellus cayanus*	SA	–
Black-fronted Dotterel	*Elseyornis melanops*	Au, Oc	Mo	Southern Lapwing	*Vanellus chilensis*	SA	Mo
Northern Lapwing	*Vanellus vanellus*	Eu, As	Pg	Andean Lapwing	*Vanellus resplendens*	SA	–
Long-toed Lapwing	*Vanellus crassirostris*	Af	Mo				
Yellow-wattled Lapwing	*Vanellus malabaricus*	As	Mo				
Banded Lapwing	*Vanellus tricolor*	Au	Mo				

Table 2: The Extinct, Critical, Endangered, and Vulnerable Shorebirds of the World (26 species).

A further 12 species are threatened.

English name	Latin name	Breeding area	Population Size (number of adults)	Conservation status
Canarian Black Oystercatcher	*Haematopus meadewaldoi*	Africa	-	Extinct
White-winged Sandpiper	*Prosobonia leucoptera*	Oceania	-	Extinct
Javanese Wattled Lapwing	*Vanellus macropterus*	Asia	-	Extinct
Eskimo Curlew	*Numenius borealis*	North America	c.50	Critical
Slender-billed Curlew	*Numenius tenuirostris*	Asia	c.50	Critical
Black Stilt	*Himantopus novaezelandiae*	New Zealand	c.60	Critical
Nordmann's Greenshank	*Tringa guttifer*	Asia	c.1,000	Endangered
Tuamotu Sandpiper	*Prosobonia cancellata*	Oceania	190-250	Endangered
Red-breasted Plover	*Charadrius obscurus*	Oceania	c. 60	Endangered
St Helena Plover	*Charadrius sanctaehelenae*	Africa	c.315	Endangered
Shore Plover	*Charadrius novaeseelandiae*	Oceania	c.130	Endangered
Plains-wanderer	*Pedionomus torquatus*	Australia	11,000	Vulnerable
Amami Woodcock	*Scolopax mira*	Asia	< 10,000	Vulnerable
Moluccan Woodcock	*Scolopax rochussenii*	Asia	?	Vulnerable
Solitary Snipe	*Gallinago solitaria*	Asia	?	Vulnerable
Wood Snipe	*Gallinago nemoricola*	Asia	?	Vulnerable
Chatham Snipe	*Coenocorypha pusilla*	Oceania	c.1,000	Vulnerable
Bristle-thighed Curlew	*Numenius tahitiensis*	North America	< 10,000	Vulnerable
Spoon-billed Sandpiper	*Eurynorhynchus pygmaeus*	Asia	2,000-2,800	Vulnerable
Broad-billed Sandpiper	*Limicola falcinellus*	Europe, Asia	26,000-44,000	Vulnerable
Black-banded Plover	*Charadrius thoracicus*	Africa	< 1,000	Vulnerable
Piping Plover	*Charadrius melodus*	North America	c.3,000	Vulnerable
Mountain Plover	*Charadrius montanus*	North America	5,000-10,000	Vulnerable
Hooded Plover	*Charadrius rubricollis*	Australia	> 5,000	Vulnerable
Wrybill	*Anarhynchus frontalis*	Oceania	c.5,000	Vulnerable
Sociable Lapwing	*Vanellus gregarius*	Europe, Asia	(< 5,000?)	Vulnerable

Conservation Status:
Critical - (verging on extinction);
Endangered - (global population in large decline and fewer than 10,000 breeding pairs);
Vulnerable - (global population in large decline with more than 10,000 pairs, or in moderate decline and fewer than 10,000 pairs).
Near threatened species (declining in many parts of their range): Sulawesi woodcock, Latham's snipe, great snipe, Fuegian snipe, imperial snipe, subantartic snipe, Hudsonian godwit, far eastern curlew, Asian dowitcher, African black oystercatcher, diademed plover and Magellanic plover
Population size: ? = not known

Index

*Entries in **bold** indicate pictures*

Recommended Reading and Biographical Note

Hayman, P., Marchant, J., & Prater, T. (1998, reprint). *Shorebirds. An identification guide to the Waders of the World.* London and Boston. A superb guide to identification, distribution and habits.

Hoyo, del, J., Elliott, A., & Sargatal, J. (eds) (1996). *Handbook of the Birds of the World.* Vol. 3. Hoatzin to Auks. Barcelona. An up-to-date standard general reference (821 pages), with much of the shorebird text written by Theunis Piersma and Popko Wiersma.

Matthiessen, Peter. (1967). *The Shorebirds of North America.* (edited by G.D. Stout). New York. An evocative text, with magnificent paintings by Robert Verity Clem.

Piersma, T., Wiersma, P., and van Gils, J. (1997). The many unknowns about plovers and sandpipers of the world: introduction to a wealth of research opportunities highly relevant for shorebird conservation. *Wader Study Group Bulletin*, 82: 22-33. An important paper.

Wader Study Group Bulletin and *International Wader Studies,*
produced by the Wader Study Group, an association of amateurs and professionals from all over the world. Details from: WSG, c/o National Centre for Ornithology, The Nunnery, Thetford, Norfolk IP24 2PU, UK. www. uct.ac.za/depts/stats/adu/wsg

This is the authors' second book, following their highly acclaimed *Tundra Plovers*, published in the Poyser/Academic Press series in 1998.

Prof Des Thompson is with Scottish Natural Heritage, where he works on upland and conservation issues. He has produced six books, and is an Associate Editor of *Ibis* (one of the leading scientific journals on birds). Dr Ingvar Byrkjedal is Curator of Vertebrates at the Zoological Museum, University of Bergen, Norway. He has researched shorebirds in the new and old worlds, especially in tundra regions, and is the world expert on several of these. The authors share a passion for shorebirds, and especially their northern haunts.